Table of Contents

Introduction 14

   History of AMEL: 15

      Emergence of Monitoring and Evaluation (M&E): ... 16

      Focus on Accountability 16

      Learning and Knowledge Management 16

      Integration of AMEL 17

      Participatory Approaches 17

      Focus on Theory of Change 18

      Technological Advancements 18

Accountability 19

   Examples of responsibility in action 20

   Characteristics of the reporting obligation 23

AMEL (1)

Accountability mechanisms 24

Principles of responsibility 25

Accountability Vs. Responsibility 26

The Power of Accountability 27

    Fostering a Culture of Responsibility in the Workplace: 27

    The Significance of Accountability: 28

    Understanding Accountability: 29

    Building a Culture of Responsibility: 29

The Role of Accountability in the Monetary World 33

    Demonstrating Responsibility in Action: 33

    Auditor Responsibility: 33

    External Accountants and Audit Committees: 34

- Employee Accountability: ...35
- Corporate Responsibility: ...36
- Accountability and Transparency in Corporate Governance: ...37
- Significance of accountability in different contexts: ...38
  - Accountability in Government and Public Sector: ...38
  - Social Accountability: ...38
  - Environmental Accountability: ...39
  - Professional and Ethical Accountability: ...40
  - Financial Accountability: ...40
  - Personal Accountability: ...41
- Understanding the Dynamics of Reporting Obligations 42
  - Characteristics of Responsibility: ...43

Accountability Mechanisms: 44

Reporting Mechanisms Across the Organization: 45

Strengthening Leadership Engagement: 46

Clearly Defined Responsibility and Power: 48

Provision of Advice and Support: 48

Accountability in Leadership: 49

Understanding the Distinction: 50

Implications in Organizational and Project Management: 51

Balancing Responsibility and Accountability: 51

Responsibility and accountability in leadership: 53

Responsibility: 53

Task-oriented approach 53

Decision-making..53

Delegation and empowerment............................53

Communication and coordination 54

Transparency and integrity 54

Stakeholder relationships 55

Performance evaluation 55

Learning and growth 55

Mutual Reinforcement: 56

Accountability strengthens responsibility...............56

Both responsibility and accountability contribute to trust-building 56

The combination of responsibility and accountability leads to organizational effectiveness 57

Enhancing Program Effectiveness through Comprehensive Monitoring and Evaluation: 58

Understanding Surveillance 59

The Continuous Nature of Monitoring and Evaluation 59

Monitoring and Evaluation 60

Monitoring and Assessment................................61

Taking Appropriate Action 61

Application of the Principles.................................62

Clearly defined job descriptions and roles 62

Performance management systems 62

Training and development programs 63

Transparent communication channels.................63

Compliance frameworks 63

Continuous improvement initiatives 63

Exploring the Distinction between Accountability and Responsibility in Leadership 64

Responsibility in Leadership 65

What is surveillance? 65

When to watch 66

What to watch out for 67

What to watch and evaluate 67

Outputs 67

Results 68

Effect 68

Types of monitoring 68

- Objective of monitoring 69
- The Role of Monitoring and Evaluation: 73
  - Assessing program effectiveness 73
  - Monitoring program costs 74
  - Facilitating informed decision-making 74
  - Enhancing accountability 74
- Integrating Monitoring and Evaluation into Program Design 75
- Enhancing Program Evaluation: 76
  - Maximizing Impact and Accountability: 76
  - Evaluating Program Impact: 77
  - Measuring Results and Changes: 77
- Benefits for Stakeholders: 79

Beneficiaries 79

Employees 79

Executive Leadership 79

Donors 80

Enhancing Learning and Accountability in Monitoring, Evaluation, and Accountability 81

Learning 81

Learning and Responsibility 84

Integration of Learning into the Evaluation Process . 85

Developing Comprehensive Theories of Social Change 85

Evaluating Participatory Projects: 86

Learning as a Tool for Various Stakeholders: 87

Enhancing Fiscal Policies through Learning: 87

The Role of AMEL in Sustainable Development: 89

Unveiling the Pillars of Sustainable Development 89

The Interplay of Accountability, Monitoring, Evaluation and Learning in Sustainable Development 93

Monitoring for Sustainable Development 94

Designing Effective Monitoring Systems:..............95

Case Studies in Monitoring for Sustainable Development 96

Evaluation as a Catalyst for Sustainable Development 98

Evaluating Sustainable Development Programs: 99

Methods, Approaches, and Frameworks 99

Utilizing Evaluation Results: 101

Informing Decision-Making and Improving Effectiveness...............101

Real-Life Examples of Evaluation in Sustainable Development Initiatives.................103

Accountability for Sustainable Development...........105

The Significance of Accountability: Transparency, Responsibility, and Trust................105

Mechanisms for Accountability: Stakeholder Engagement and Reporting...........107

Showcasing Accountability in Sustainable Development Efforts.......................109

Learning for Continuous Improvement in Sustainable Development....................111

The Power of Learning: Promoting Adaptation, Innovation, and Knowledge Sharing 112

Inspiring Examples of Learning in Sustainable Development Endeavors 115

Integrated Approaches: 117

Harmonizing Monitoring, Evaluation, Accountability, and Learning..117

Challenges and Considerations in Integrating AMEL in Sustainable Development...........................120

Success Stories of Integrated AMEL Approaches in Sustainable Development Practice....................121

Recommended Resources: 124

Further Readings on AMEL and Sustainable Development 124

Books 125

Reports and Publications 126

Academic Journals 127

Online Courses and Training Programs 128

Introduction

This book highlights the fundamentals, concepts and principals of the four combined subjects "Monitoring Evaluation Accountability and Learn". The author focuses on simplifying the terms and the description of the said, and to provide the most needful and useful information. Monitoring, evaluation, accountability and learning AMEL are part of day-to-day program management and are critical to the success of all programs, including those operating in fragile environments. Without effective nutrition, we cannot track progress, make adjustments, track unintended program results, or assess the impact on the lives of the people we work with. The feedback system also helps us take action against stakeholders by exchanging information and developing a grievance or feedback mechanism to guide program implementation.

History of AMEL:

The history of Accountability, Monitoring, Evaluation and Learning (AMEL) spans several decades and has evolved in response to the changing landscape of international development and aid effectiveness. The following is a brief overview of key milestones and developments in the history of AMEL:

Emergence of Monitoring and Evaluation (M&E): The origins of AMEL can be traced back to the emergence of monitoring and evaluation practices in the mid-20th century. As development programs and projects became more complex, there was a growing recognition of the need to track progress, measure outcomes, and assess the impact of interventions. M&E methodologies and frameworks began to take shape, providing a systematic approach to assessing development initiatives.

Focus on Accountability: In the 1990s, there was a significant shift toward greater accountability in the field of development. Donors, governments, and civil society organizations increasingly emphasized the need for transparency and accountability in the use of development resources. Accountability mechanisms were introduced to ensure that funds were used effectively and efficiently, and that stakeholders were involved in decision-making processes.

Learning and Knowledge Management: In the late 1990s and early 2000s, the concept of learning gained prominence in the field of AMEL. It was recognized that evaluation should not only focus on accountability but also serve as a tool for learning and knowledge management. The importance of capturing and disseminating lessons learned, best practices, and evidence-based approaches became integral to improving the effectiveness of development interventions.

Integration of AMEL: As the understanding of AMEL evolved, there was a growing recognition of the need to integrate Accountability, Monitoring, Evaluation and Learning into a cohesive framework. The integration of these components aimed to create a more holistic and comprehensive approach to assessing and improving development programs. This integration allowed for a continuous feedback loop, where data and insights from monitoring and evaluation informed decision-making, while accountability mechanisms ensured transparency and learning facilitated adaptive management.

Participatory Approaches: Another significant development in the history of AMEL was the increased emphasis on participatory approaches. Recognizing the importance of including stakeholders, especially beneficiaries, in the evaluation process, participatory methods were widely adopted. This shift aimed to empower communities, promote ownership, and ensure that evaluation findings and recommendations were contextually relevant and actionable.

Focus on Theory of Change: In recent years, there has been a growing focus on developing theories of change within the AMEL framework. Theories of change provide a comprehensive understanding of how interventions are expected to lead to desired outcomes and impact. By incorporating theories of change into the evaluation process, organizations can better assess the relevance and effectiveness of their interventions and make informed adjustments as needed.

Technological Advancements: Advancements in technology have significantly influenced the practice of AMEL. The use of digital tools, data collection platforms, and information management systems has revolutionized data collection, analysis, and reporting processes. These technological innovations have enabled more efficient and timely data collection, improved data quality, and facilitated real-time monitoring and evaluation.

The history of AMEL is marked by the evolution of monitoring and evaluation practices, the increasing emphasis on accountability, the integration of learning and knowledge management, the adoption of participatory approaches, the focus on theories of change, and the impact of technological advancements. As the field continues to evolve, AMEL will play a vital role in enhancing the effectiveness and impact of development interventions.

Accountability

Accountability means when a person or grouped entity manages some consequences or activities. It is essential for all stakeholders. If accountability is absent, it will become very hard to find people responsible for their actions because they feel that they have no consequences. Successful teams cannot be managed without accountability results and responsibilities are inextricably linked. Creating a culture of corporate exposure is often the secret of successful teams. This promotes better working relationships, improves job performance and eliminates surprises. Why is the concept of responsibility often loaded with negative undertones, anxiety and even fear?

The reason is that we use this concept as a disciplinary procedure if something is wrong with someone's property guilt. Have you ever worked in a location that is traditionally hit with late deadlines, breaking promises or teammates to comply with the rules and breaking? It was probably the organization where the trust level was low and the strategy had no accountability. The first step in the workplace to promote a culture of responsibility is to understand and reintegrate what it means.

Examples of responsibility in action

There are many examples of how the monetary world seeks to implement accountability. The auditor audited by the financial statements of the Company is responsible for obtaining reasonable assurance that there are no material misstatements caused by errors or fraud. Liability requires the accountant to be careful and aware of his or her professional practices, as even negligence can lead to legal liability. For example, the accountant is responsible for the integrity and accuracy of financial statements, even if he has not made any mistakes. Business owners can try to manage their company's financial statements without knowing this accountant. Managers have a clear incentive to do this, as their salary is usually linked to the performance of the company. Therefore, independent external accountants must audit the accounts and their responsibility requires them to be careful and conscientious. Activities should also constitute the audit committee in their calculation, which is not subject to accounting institutions. Their goal is to control and revise. Accountability is the assurance that an individual or organization is evaluated for their performance or behavior associated with something for which they are responsible. This term is related to responsibility, but is revisited more from the point of view of supervision. An employee may be responsible, for example, for complying with the request to comply with all required requirements. If the job is not satisfactory, the consequences may or may not be. Accountability, on the other hand, means that the employee is responsible for the proper execution of the project and must at least explain why he did not do it. Corporate responsibility includes the responsibility of all stakeholders in the organization for all activities and results. For example, through the Performance and Report, it compiles and documents organizational factors that quantify the profitability, efficiency and budget of the reservation against the actual results of the original objectives. The performance report procedure is usually performed once during exercise, although in some cases it becomes more frequent. Corporate responsibility also means that the organization should be accountable for any deviation from its own goals and values which can be documented and made available to the public through a mission or vision. In addition, the concept of corporate responsibility is often extended to require companies to adhere to ethical, responsible and sustainable practices. Accountability and transparency are generally considered good corporate governance in two main cells.

Characteristics of the reporting obligation

Responsibility can be characterized in several ways. Responsibility is personal, which means that powers can only be delegated to one person. Responsibility is vertical, i.e., from top to bottom, responsibilities and powers are transferred from the supervisor to the subordinate the supervisor must therefore be secondary. Responsibility is neutral, that is, it is not a positive or negative concept. Excellent results are recognized, but failure can result in penalties, including rolling back or modifying operating systems. The four principles of accountability require a clear definition of responsibilities and principles, the provision of guidance and support to all stakeholders at all stages, the use of responsibilities and principles to be monitored and evaluated, and appropriate action taken.

Accountability mechanisms

There are different types of NGO reporting mechanisms. For example, they include documents such as legal instruments, policies, mandates, values, laws, rules and regulations. It can also take the form of processes involving labor, disbursement and resource mobilization and accounting, etc. At some point, internal and external teams will be put in place to monitor and review NGO responsibilities. There are policies that include goal setting, job scheduling, and performance reporting. Liability also includes the legal system filing a complaint against law enforcement, etc. There are several reporting mechanisms across the organization, such as program management planning and review, management oversight of compliance audits, and accountability committees that have been put in place. Program management planning and review includes issues such as improving the performance appraisal system of NGO leaders, NGO leaders reporting directly to the board or council, leadership engagement NGOs to achieve measurable goals or an overview of achievements of the previous year for subsequent years.

Principles of responsibility

What are the basic principles of NGO accountability and how can it be applied? One of the first principles is that responsibility and power must be clearly defined. The manager must be informed of the expected results of the program and of the financial and human resources at his disposal. Monitoring and evaluation systems need to be clarified, as well as organizational values, policies, rules and regulations and standards of conduct. The second principle requires the provision of advice and support to the responsible person in the form of regular and timely information on management, training and development, access to senior management and management experts, financial and human resources. The third principle requires monitoring and assessing the needs for accountability and authority. To this end, an objective comparison of results with targets and standards should be made, covering issues such as program delivery, cost and quality, human and financial resource management, decision making the mandate is fully exercised but not exceeded and adherence to policies, values, rules, regulations and standards of conduct. The last principle is to take the appropriate action. He is facing problems like excellence, satisfactory performance, and unsatisfactory performance in responsibility and power due to negligence or ignorance, improper execution of responsibility and power due to intentional denial of policies, rules and regulations, or overstepping of decision-making boundaries.

Accountability Vs. Responsibility

The main difference between responsibility and accountability is that accountability focuses only on taking ownership of work-related actions and decisions, while accountability is often a task assigned to you by higher authority.

A leader is someone who guides others to do the best they can for a particular task. Therefore, a good leader should have leadership qualities such as empowerment, responsibility, task knowledge, leadership skills, etc. Responsibility and accountability for what has been assigned to you means that you will be recognized and accepted as being able to perform this task. Moreover, you will be recognized as able to be a good example and a good guide for those who follow your path. Accountability and responsibility are often used interchangeably, but have different meanings. Thus, a manager must understand the difference between accountability and responsibility whether the organization, the project, etc. will perform its functions to the best of its ability.

The Power of Accountability

Fostering a Culture of Responsibility in the Workplace:

Accountability plays a crucial role in organizations, ensuring that individuals and groups take ownership of their actions and accept the consequences. It is a fundamental principle that is essential for all stakeholders involved. In the absence of accountability, it becomes challenging to hold individuals responsible for their actions, as they perceive a lack of consequences. Successful teams rely on accountability to achieve results and fulfill their responsibilities. By creating a culture of corporate exposure, teams can foster better working relationships, enhance job performance, and eliminate surprises. However, the concept of accountability is often burdened with negative undertones, anxiety, and fear. In this article, we will explore the importance of accountability in the workplace, its impact on organizational culture, and strategies to promote a culture of responsibility.

The Significance of Accountability:

Accountability serves as the cornerstone of a well-functioning organization. It establishes a framework where individuals are answerable for their actions, decisions, and outcomes. It creates a sense of ownership and responsibility, driving individuals to perform their tasks diligently and with integrity. In a workplace that lacks accountability, trust levels tend to be low, deadlines are frequently missed, promises are broken, and team members may disregard rules and regulations. This breeds a culture of complacency and undermines the overall success of the organization.

Understanding Accountability:

To promote a culture of responsibility, it is crucial to redefine and reintegrate the concept of accountability. Often, accountability is associated solely with disciplinary procedures and assigning blame when something goes wrong. However, this limited perspective hinders its positive potential. Accountability should be viewed as a proactive and empowering force that encourages individuals to take ownership of their actions, learn from their mistakes, and strive for continuous improvement. By reframing accountability in this way, organizations can foster a positive environment that supports growth and development.

Building a Culture of Responsibility:

Clear Expectations and Goals: Establishing clear expectations and goals is vital to ensure accountability. When individuals have a clear understanding of what is expected of them, they are more likely to take ownership of their responsibilities. Clear communication of objectives, deadlines, and performance metrics provides a roadmap for success and enables individuals to track their progress effectively.

Empowerment and Autonomy: Empowering employees and granting them autonomy can significantly enhance accountability. When individuals have a sense of ownership and control over their work, they are more likely to take personal responsibility for their actions. This can be achieved by delegating tasks, encouraging decision-making, and fostering a culture of trust and respect.

Continuous Feedback and Coaching: Regular feedback and coaching sessions are essential to promote accountability. Providing constructive feedback helps individuals understand their strengths and areas for improvement, allowing them to take corrective actions. Coaching sessions can also serve as an opportunity to align goals, address challenges, and provide support when needed.

Transparent Communication: Open and transparent communication is a cornerstone of accountability. It encourages individuals to share their ideas, concerns, and progress openly. Transparent communication also ensures that expectations, responsibilities, and outcomes are clearly understood by all team members, promoting a shared sense of accountability.

Recognition and Rewards: Recognizing and rewarding individuals for their accountable behavior reinforces the desired culture. Celebrating achievements and acknowledging individuals who consistently demonstrate responsibility creates a positive work environment and motivates others to follow suit. By linking accountability to positive outcomes, organizations can cultivate a culture that values responsibility.

Lead by Example: Leaders play a crucial role in shaping the culture of accountability. When leaders model accountable behavior, it sets the tone for the entire organization. Leaders should demonstrate integrity, take responsibility for their actions, and hold themselves accountable to the same standards they expect from their teams. Leading by example fosters trust, inspires others, and strengthens the culture of responsibility.

Accountability is a foundational element of organizational success. It promotes a culture of responsibility, transparency, and trust, driving individuals and teams to perform at their best. By redefining accountability as a proactive and empowering force, organizations can create an environment where individuals take ownership of their actions, learn from their mistakes, and strive for continuous improvement. Implementing strategies such as setting clear expectations, empowering employees, providing feedback, fostering transparent communication, recognizing accountable behavior, and leading by example can help organizations foster a culture of responsibility and reap its numerous benefits.

The Role of Accountability in the Monetary World

Demonstrating Responsibility in Action:

AMEL (31)

Accountability is a fundamental aspect of the monetary world, ensuring that individuals and organizations are held responsible for their actions and behaviors. In this article, we will explore various examples of how accountability is implemented in the financial sector. From auditors ensuring the integrity of financial statements to corporate responsibility encompassing ethical practices, we will delve into the significance of responsibility in action.

Auditor Responsibility:

Auditors play a crucial role in ensuring the accuracy and reliability of financial statements. Their responsibility is to obtain reasonable assurance that there are no material misstatements caused by errors or fraud. This requires auditors to be diligent, cautious, and aware of professional practices. Even the slightest negligence on their part can lead to legal liability. For instance, auditors are accountable for the integrity and accuracy of financial statements, irrespective of whether they personally made any mistakes. This accountability is essential as it provides stakeholders with confidence in the financial information presented by companies.

External Accountants and Audit Committees:

Business owners may attempt to manage their company's financial statements without involving independent external accountants. However, there is a clear incentive for managers to do so, as their salary is often linked to the company's performance. To ensure transparency and accountability, independent external accountants are appointed to audit the accounts. Their responsibility lies in conducting a thorough examination, identifying any discrepancies, and providing an unbiased assessment. The accountability of external accountants requires them to exercise due care and professionalism in their work. Additionally, organizations can establish audit committees comprised of individuals who are not affiliated with the accounting institution. These committees aim to enhance control, oversight, and accountability in financial reporting processes.

Employee Accountability:

Accountability extends beyond the financial realm and encompasses the responsibility of employees within an organization. Employees may be responsible for fulfilling specific job requirements or complying with certain requests. However, accountability goes a step further by ensuring that employees are answerable for the proper execution of their tasks. If an employee fails to meet expectations, accountability requires them to provide an explanation for their actions or inactions. This level of accountability promotes transparency, encourages a culture of responsibility, and fosters continuous improvement within the workforce.

Corporate Responsibility:

Corporate responsibility encompasses the accountability of all stakeholders within an organization for its activities and outcomes. Performance reporting plays a significant role in documenting and evaluating organizational factors such as profitability, efficiency, and budget adherence. By comparing actual results against the original objectives, performance reports enable organizations to assess their performance and identify deviations. Corporate responsibility also entails aligning the organization's actions with its stated goals and values, which are often documented and made available to the public through mission or vision statements. Furthermore, the concept of corporate responsibility extends to encompass ethical, responsible, and sustainable practices, ensuring that organizations operate in a manner that benefits society and the environment.

Accountability and Transparency in Corporate Governance:

Accountability and transparency are fundamental principles of good corporate governance. Accountability ensures that individuals and organizations are held responsible for their actions and decisions. It fosters transparency by requiring the disclosure of relevant information, enabling stakeholders to make informed decisions. By adhering to these principles, organizations can build trust, enhance their reputation, and maintain the confidence of their stakeholders.

Accountability is integral to the monetary world, promoting responsible behavior, transparency, and trust. From auditors ensuring the accuracy of financial statements to employees taking ownership of their tasks, accountability is demonstrated at various levels. Corporate responsibility further expands the notion of accountability by encompassing the responsibility of all stakeholders, including adherence to ethical and sustainable practices. By upholding accountability and embracing transparency, organizations can foster a culture of responsibility, improve their performance, and contribute to the overall well-being of society.

Significance of accountability in different contexts:

Accountability in Government and Public Sector:

Accountability is crucial in government and the public sector to ensure transparency, prevent corruption, and promote responsible governance.

Elected officials and public servants are accountable to the citizens they serve. This accountability is manifested through mechanisms such as elections, public hearings, and oversight bodies. By holding government officials accountable for their actions and decisions, citizens can trust that their interests are being represented and that public resources are being managed responsibly.

Social Accountability:

Social accountability refers to the involvement of citizens and civil society in holding institutions accountable for their actions. It empowers individuals and communities to actively participate in decision-making processes and demand transparency and responsiveness from public and private entities. Social accountability mechanisms include citizen feedback platforms, community scorecards, and public hearings. By promoting social accountability, societies can foster a culture of active citizenship and ensure that institutions are responsive to the needs and aspirations of the people they serve.

Environmental Accountability:

In recent years, there has been a growing emphasis on environmental accountability. This involves holding individuals, organizations, and governments responsible for their impact on the environment. Environmental accountability encompasses practices such as sustainable resource management, reducing carbon emissions, and adopting environmentally friendly technologies. Through regulatory frameworks, reporting requirements, and public scrutiny, environmental accountability aims to mitigate the negative effects of human activities on the planet and promote sustainable development.

Professional and Ethical Accountability:

Accountability is also prevalent in various professions and industries, where individuals are held accountable for their professional conduct and adherence to ethical standards. For example, in the medical field, doctors are accountable for providing quality care, maintaining patient confidentiality, and upholding ethical principles. Similarly, lawyers have a responsibility to act in the best interests of their clients while respecting legal and ethical guidelines. Professional and ethical accountability ensures that practitioners uphold high standards, prioritize the well-being of those they serve, and maintain public trust in their respective fields.

Financial Accountability:

Accountability is particularly significant in the financial sector, given its impact on economies and individuals' livelihoods. Financial institutions, such as banks and investment firms, have a responsibility to manage funds responsibly, safeguard customer assets, and comply with regulatory requirements. Regulatory bodies, such as central banks and financial watchdogs, play a crucial role in enforcing accountability and ensuring the stability and integrity of financial systems. In the wake of financial crises, there has been a heightened focus on holding financial institutions accountable for their actions and promoting ethical practices in the industry.

Personal Accountability:

At an individual level, accountability is essential for personal growth and success. Taking personal responsibility for one's actions and decisions enables individuals to learn from their mistakes, make positive changes, and achieve their goals. Personal accountability involves being self-aware, setting realistic expectations, and following through on commitments. By embracing personal accountability, individuals can enhance their relationships, improve their performance, and contribute to a positive and productive society.

Accountability is a foundational principle that permeates various aspects of society. From government and public sector accountability to professional, environmental, and personal accountability, it plays a vital role in promoting responsible behavior, transparency, and trust. By holding individuals, organizations, and institutions accountable, we can foster a culture of integrity, ensure equitable outcomes, and create a better future for all.

AMEL (40)

Understanding the Dynamics of Reporting Obligations

Reporting obligations play a crucial role in establishing accountability within organizations. In this article, we will explore the characteristics of reporting obligations and delve into the various mechanisms that facilitate accountability. From the principles of responsibility to the different types of reporting mechanisms, we will provide a comprehensive analysis of this important aspect of organizational governance.

Characteristics of Responsibility:

Responsibility can be characterized by several key attributes. Firstly, responsibility is personal, meaning that it can only be delegated to an individual. This ensures that there is a clear line of accountability for actions and decisions. Secondly, responsibility is vertical, flowing from top to bottom within an organization. The transfer of responsibilities and powers occurs from supervisors to subordinates, creating a hierarchical structure that facilitates effective governance. Thirdly, responsibility is neutral, devoid of positive or negative connotations. While excellent results are recognized and rewarded, failures can lead to penalties, necessitating corrective actions and modifications to operating systems. Finally, the four principles of accountability—clear definition of responsibilities, guidance and support for stakeholders, monitoring and evaluation, and appropriate action—form the foundation of an effective reporting obligation framework.

Accountability Mechanisms:

There are various mechanisms through which accountability is ensured within organizations, particularly non-governmental organizations (NGOs). These mechanisms encompass a range of documents, processes, and oversight structures. Legal instruments, policies, mandates, values, laws, rules, and regulations form part of the reporting mechanisms. They provide a framework for organizations to operate within specific guidelines and regulations. Additionally, processes such as labor management, resource mobilization, disbursement, and accounting contribute to accountability. Internal and external teams are often established to monitor and review the responsibilities of NGOs. These teams play a crucial role in ensuring compliance and evaluating the effectiveness of reporting obligations. Furthermore, accountability mechanisms include the legal system, where complaints can be filed against organizations that fail to fulfill their obligations. This legal recourse acts as a deterrent and reinforces the importance of accountability.

Reporting Mechanisms Across the Organization:

Within an organization, there are several reporting mechanisms that facilitate accountability. Program management planning and review form an integral part of this process. It involves activities such as goal setting, job scheduling, and performance reporting. Through program management planning and review, organizations can set clear objectives, monitor progress, and assess the impact of their programs. Another important aspect of reporting obligations is management oversight of compliance audits. This ensures that organizations adhere to internal policies and external regulations. Compliance audits provide an independent assessment of an organization's adherence to reporting obligations, identifying areas for improvement and ensuring transparency. Additionally, accountability committees are often established to oversee the implementation of reporting obligations. These committees comprise individuals with diverse expertise and serve as a forum for discussions, evaluations, and recommendations related to accountability.

Strengthening Leadership Engagement:

Effective reporting obligations require strong leadership engagement. NGO leaders play a pivotal role in ensuring accountability throughout the organization. Measures can be implemented to enhance the performance appraisal system of NGO leaders, ensuring that they are evaluated based on their adherence to reporting obligations. Moreover, NGO leaders should have a direct reporting line to the board or council, facilitating transparency and direct oversight. Leadership engagement can also be fostered through the establishment of measurable goals and targets for NGOs, allowing for a clear assessment of achievements. Additionally, reviewing the accomplishments of the previous year and using them as a foundation for subsequent years enables organizations to track progress and ensure continuous improvement.

Reporting obligations are essential for establishing accountability within organizations. By understanding the characteristics of responsibility and implementing effective accountability mechanisms, organizations can promote transparency, adherence to regulations, and responsible governance. Clear definition of responsibilities, guidance and support for stakeholders, monitoring and evaluation, and appropriate actions form the basis of a robust reporting obligation framework. Through program management planning and review, management oversight of compliance audits, and the establishment of accountability committees, organizations can ensure accountability at various levels. By strengthening leadership engagement and fostering a culture of responsibility, organizations can create an environment that values accountability and drives positive change.

Key Principles of NGO Accountability and Their Application in Practice

NGO accountability is essential for ensuring effective governance and responsible management of resources. In this article, we will explore the fundamental principles of NGO accountability and examine how they can be applied. From clearly defined responsibilities and provision of support to monitoring and appropriate actions, understanding and implementing these principles is crucial for fostering transparency and achieving organizational objectives.

Clearly Defined Responsibility and Power:

The first principle of NGO accountability revolves around the clear definition of responsibility and power. It is crucial for managers to have a comprehensive understanding of their expected program results and the resources available to them, both in terms of finances and human capital. This clarity helps establish a foundation for accountability, as managers can align their actions with organizational goals and objectives. Additionally, defining monitoring and evaluation systems, organizational values, policies, rules, regulations, and standards of conduct provides a framework within which accountability can be effectively implemented.

Provision of Advice and Support:

The second principle emphasizes the importance of providing guidance and support to individuals responsible for carrying out their duties. This support can be in the form of regular and timely information on management practices, training and development opportunities, access to senior management and subject matter experts, as well as adequate financial and human resources. By equipping responsible individuals with the necessary tools and knowledge, organizations enable them to fulfill their duties effectively and navigate the complexities of their roles. This principle promotes a culture of learning and growth, enhancing accountability at all levels.

Accountability in Leadership:

Accountability goes beyond mere responsibility and involves answerability and justification for one's actions and decisions. It is the acknowledgment that as a leader, one is answerable to stakeholders for the outcomes and impact of their leadership. A leader who is accountable takes ownership not only of their own actions but also of the overall performance of the organization or project they are leading. Accountability encompasses transparency, integrity, and the willingness to accept praise or criticism for the results achieved. An accountable leader ensures that appropriate systems are in place to monitor progress, evaluates performance, and takes corrective actions when necessary. By being accountable, leaders foster trust, enhance organizational effectiveness, and build strong relationships with stakeholders.

Understanding the Distinction:

While responsibility and accountability are closely related, it is essential to recognize their differences. Responsibility is the obligation to fulfill assigned tasks, while accountability involves being answerable for the outcomes and impact of those tasks. Responsibility focuses on the individual's role, while accountability extends to the broader implications and consequences of their actions. A responsible leader performs their duties diligently, while an accountable leader takes ownership of the results, learns from successes and failures, and ensures that appropriate measures are in place to drive continuous improvement.

Implications in Organizational and Project Management:

In organizational and project management contexts, the distinction between accountability and responsibility holds significant implications. A leader who understands the difference can promote a culture of accountability and responsibility within their team or organization. By clearly defining roles and tasks, assigning responsibilities, and empowering team members, leaders can foster a sense of ownership and commitment. Additionally, establishing mechanisms for monitoring progress, evaluating performance, and providing feedback enables leaders to hold themselves and their team members accountable for the results achieved. This accountability-driven approach enhances transparency, improves decision-making, and ensures that organizational goals are met effectively.

Balancing Responsibility and Accountability:

Effective leaders strike a balance between responsibility and accountability. They not only fulfill their assigned tasks but also take ownership of the broader outcomes and impact of their leadership. By assuming responsibility, leaders demonstrate reliability and gain the trust of their team members. Simultaneously, by embracing accountability, leaders create a culture of transparency, continuous improvement, and learning. This balance promotes a positive work environment, encourages innovation, and drives organizational success.

In leadership, responsibility and accountability are two distinct but interconnected concepts. Responsibility refers to fulfilling assigned tasks, while accountability involves answering for the outcomes and impact of those tasks. Understanding the difference between these terms is crucial for leaders to effectively guide their teams and organizations. By embracing responsibility and accountability, leaders can set a positive example, inspire their followers, and drive success. Balancing these qualities ensures that leaders not only fulfill their obligations but also take ownership of the overall performance and outcomes, fostering a culture of transparency, continuous improvement, and responsible leadership.

Responsibility and accountability in leadership:

Responsibility:

Responsibility in leadership encompasses various aspects:

Task-oriented approach: Leaders with a strong sense of responsibility focus on delivering results and meeting objectives. They ensure that tasks are completed efficiently, deadlines are met, and resources are utilized effectively.

Decision-making: Responsible leaders make informed decisions by considering all relevant factors and evaluating potential risks and benefits. They take ownership of their decisions and are willing to be held accountable for the consequences.

Delegation and empowerment: Effective leaders delegate tasks to team members while providing clear instructions and expectations. They empower others to take responsibility for their assigned roles and encourage autonomy and initiative.

Communication and coordination: Responsible leaders maintain open lines of communication with their team members, ensuring clarity on goals, expectations, and progress. They coordinate efforts, address challenges, and provide guidance to ensure collective responsibility.

"

Accountability adds an additional layer to leadership by focusing on the outcomes and impact of actions:

"

Transparency and integrity: Accountable leaders operate with transparency, ensuring that information is shared openly and honestly. They display integrity by following through on commitments, admitting mistakes, and taking corrective actions when necessary.

Stakeholder relationships: Accountable leaders foster strong relationships with stakeholders, such as team members, clients, partners, and the wider community. They proactively engage with stakeholders, communicate progress, and seek feedback to improve performance.

Performance evaluation: Accountable leaders establish systems to monitor and evaluate performance against established goals and targets. They analyze results, identify areas for improvement, and take necessary steps to enhance performance and achieve desired outcomes.

Learning and growth: Accountable leaders view setbacks and failures as opportunities for learning and growth. They encourage a culture of continuous improvement, innovation, and knowledge sharing within the organization.

Mutual Reinforcement:

"

Responsibility and accountability are interconnected and mutually reinforcing:

"

Responsibility lays the foundation for accountability. When leaders take responsibility for their actions, they set an example for their team members to do the same. This creates a culture of ownership and commitment throughout the organization.

Accountability strengthens responsibility: When leaders hold themselves and others accountable, it promotes a sense of urgency, attention to detail, and a focus on delivering high-quality results.

Both responsibility and accountability contribute to trust-building: When leaders fulfill their responsibilities and are accountable for their actions, it builds trust among team members, stakeholders, and the wider community. Trust is essential for effective collaboration and achieving shared goals.

The combination of responsibility and accountability leads to organizational effectiveness: Leaders who balance these qualities create an environment of transparency, performance excellence, and continuous improvement, leading to increased productivity, innovation, and success.

Responsibility and accountability are integral components of effective leadership. Responsible leaders fulfill their assigned tasks, make informed decisions, delegate effectively, and maintain open communication. Accountable leaders go beyond responsibility by taking ownership of outcomes, maintaining transparency, and fostering stakeholder relationships. When responsibility and accountability are embraced and balanced, leaders inspire their teams, build trust, and drive organizational success. By cultivating these qualities, leaders create a culture of excellence, innovation, and continuous improvement, positioning their organizations for long-term growth and achievement.

Enhancing Program Effectiveness through Comprehensive Monitoring and Evaluation:

Monitoring and evaluation (M&E) play a crucial role in assessing the effectiveness of programs and interventions. By combining data collection and analysis, M&E provides valuable insights into whether objectives are being met and helps identify areas for improvement. However, traditional approaches to M&E have often been time-consuming and limited to reporting results, focusing solely on impact assessments. In this article, we will explore the significance of monitoring and evaluation in program management, the concept of surveillance, and the importance of integrating M&E into the program design. Furthermore, we will discuss the continuous nature of M&E, its role in decision-making, and the need for comprehensive planning and resource allocation.

Understanding Surveillance: Surveillance, in the context of M&E, refers to the periodic monitoring of activities through systematic data collection and analysis. It involves tracking the progress of each activity on a daily, weekly, monthly, quarterly, and annual basis. The primary objective of surveillance is to assess whether the program or intervention is being implemented effectively and to identify any deviations from the intended course. Surveillance involves identifying the target group or beneficiaries, determining the activities being implemented, and ensuring that they are aligned with the program's goals. By monitoring these factors, organizations can gather valuable information and measure progress towards desired outcomes.

The Continuous Nature of Monitoring and Evaluation: M&E is not a one-time event but a continuous process that should span the entire duration of a program. For effective M&E, it is essential to plan and allocate the necessary resources, including time, money, and personnel, from the program's inception. Monitoring should occur at every stage of the program, with data collection, analysis, and utilization integrated into ongoing operations. This continuous monitoring allows for timely feedback and early identification of progress or lack thereof. By providing regular updates on program performance, M&E enables management and stakeholders to make informed decisions and take corrective actions as needed. It also ensures the efficient use of resources and supports adaptive management strategies.

Monitoring and Evaluation

Monitoring and evaluation are combination of data collection and analysis to assess how well a program or intervention has or has not met its objectives evaluation. Monitoring and evaluation were used to assess the effectiveness of the project, program and social initiatives.

The vast majority of monitoring or evaluation M&E was time consuming and was limited to reporting and communicating results, which is only an impact assessment.

Monitoring and Assessment:

The third principle focuses on monitoring and assessing the accountability and authority requirements. Organizations must objectively compare results against targets and standards, covering various aspects such as program delivery, cost and quality, human and financial resource management, and adherence to policies, values, rules, regulations, and standards of conduct. This process allows for a comprehensive evaluation of performance and highlights areas that require improvement or corrective actions. Regular monitoring facilitates proactive decision-making and ensures that responsibilities and powers are exercised within the defined boundaries.

Taking Appropriate Action:

The last principle emphasizes the need for organizations to take appropriate actions based on the outcomes of monitoring and assessment processes. This involves addressing issues related to excellence, satisfactory performance, and unsatisfactory performance. In cases of negligence, ignorance, or improper execution of responsibilities and powers, appropriate action should be taken to rectify the situation. This may include providing additional support, training, or guidance to enhance performance. Similarly, intentional denial of policies, rules, and regulations or overstepping decision-making boundaries should be addressed to maintain accountability and uphold organizational standards.

Application of the Principles:

To apply these principles effectively, organizations can implement certain practices and strategies:

Clearly defined job descriptions and roles:

Ensuring that each position within the organization has a well-defined set of responsibilities and authority levels.

Performance management systems: Implementing robust systems to monitor and evaluate individual and organizational performance against predetermined targets and standards.

Training and development programs: Offering regular training opportunities to enhance skills and knowledge relevant to the roles and responsibilities of individuals within the organization.

Transparent communication channels: Establishing open lines of communication that allow for the timely sharing of information and feedback between different levels of the organization.

Compliance frameworks: Developing comprehensive frameworks that outline policies, rules, regulations, and standards of conduct, along with mechanisms to ensure adherence and address non-compliance.

Continuous improvement initiatives: Encouraging a culture of learning and innovation, where individuals are empowered to suggest improvements and contribute to the organization's overall accountability.

The principles of NGO accountability provide a framework for effective governance and responsible management. By clearly defining responsibility and power, providing advice and support, monitoring and assessing performance, and taking appropriate action, organizations can establish a culture of accountability. Through the application of these principles, NGOs can enhance transparency, improve performance, and achieve their objectives while upholding the highest ethical standards. Embracing accountability not only benefits the organization but also fosters trust and credibility among stakeholders, ultimately leading to greater impact and success in the pursuit of the organization's mission.

Exploring the Distinction between Accountability and Responsibility in Leadership

Leadership is a pivotal role that involves guiding and inspiring others to achieve their best in a given task or objective. Effective leaders possess certain qualities, including empowerment, responsibility, task knowledge, and leadership skills. Among these qualities, responsibility and accountability play a crucial role in establishing a leader's credibility and ability to perform their assigned tasks. While these terms are often used interchangeably, it is important for managers and leaders to understand their distinct meanings. This article will delve into the difference between accountability and responsibility, highlighting their significance in organizational and project management contexts and their impact on overall performance.

Responsibility in Leadership: Responsibility refers to the obligation or duty that an individual assumes when assigned a specific task or role. In leadership, taking responsibility means accepting the consequences of one's actions and decisions. A responsible leader understands the importance of fulfilling their obligations and strives to meet the expectations placed upon them. A responsible leader is reliable, dependable, and committed to delivering results. They take ownership of their tasks, allocate resources effectively, and ensure that their team members understand their roles and responsibilities. By exemplifying responsibility, leaders set a positive example for their followers and inspire them to act responsibly as well.

What is surveillance?

Definition of Periodically Monitoring of the progress of each activity daily, weekly, monthly, quarterly, annually through systematic collection and analysis of data and information is called monitoring. The target group or beneficiaries should be identified as well as what you are doing and whether your activities are being implemented or not. Monitoring a program or intervention involves the collection of routine data that measures progress towards program goals. It is also used to monitor program costs and changes in performance over time. Monitoring provides regular feedback and the first signs of progress or no progress. Its purpose is to enable management and stakeholders to make informed decisions about the effectiveness of programs and the efficient use of resources.

When to watch

M&E is a continuous process that takes place throughout the program. For mergers and acquisitions to be more effective, they must be planned at the programming stage and all the necessary resources time, money and personnel must be calculated and allocated in advance. Monitoring should take place at every stage of the program and data should be collected, analyzed and used on an ongoing basis. Typically, M&E accounts for around 10% of the total project budget. The evaluation usually takes place at the end of the programs. However, they should be programmed from the start, as they are based on data collected throughout the program, with input data being especially important.

What to watch out for

- Hierarchy level of objectives

What to watch and evaluate

- Activities
- Are planned activities completed on time and on budget? What unplanned activities have been carried out?

Outputs

What immediate material products or services did the project deliver as a result of the activity?

Results

What changes have taken place as a result of the results and to what extent they are likely to contribute to the project proposal and the desired impact.

Effect

To what extent has the project contributed to the achievement of its long-term objectives? Why or why not? What were the unexpected positive or negative consequences of the project? Why did they arrive?

Types of monitoring

- Process monitoring real-time monitoring.
- Progress monitoring.
- Validation of progress.
- Performance monitoring.

Monitoring is the ordinary registration and recording of the activities of a project or program. It is a process that regularly collects information on all aspects of the project and observing the progress of project activities. This is an observation. Monitoring also includes providing feedback to funders, implementers and beneficiaries of the project on the progress of the project. Reporting allows the information collected to be used to improve project performance in decision making.

Objective of monitoring

Monitoring is very important in the design and implementation of the project. It's like looking at a bicycle. You can adapt as you go and make sure you're on the right track. Tracking provides useful information like the analysis of the situation of the community and its work. It also helps to determine if the project inputs are being used correctly. Another objective is to identify community or project problems and find solutions and make sure the right people and all activities are done on time, using the lessons from one experience to another. And determine if designing the project is the most appropriate way to solve the problem. What is he looking at? Follow up should be periodic and continuous, after the start of the program and during or during the intervention. The data obtained is primarily based on inputs and outputs and is generally used to determine the effectiveness of the application as an ongoing strategy. For example, rejection of in school teacher training may track the number of sites they visit each month, the education provided, the number of teachers in training, etc. Key issues to consider in the surveillance strategy include what key metrics can give us an idea of the state of the application? Do we have Lean data collection and analysis procedures? How effectively are we delivering our programs? Based on the data obtained, should we make any changes to our programs? The monitoring plan usually focuses on the processes that take place during program implementation? These may include follow up during the following periods when the programs have been implemented. The location or area where the programs were offered? Which departments or groups carried out the activities? How often do certain activities take place? Number of people approached through program activities. Number of products delivered or number of services. Program implementation cost.

Program evaluation focuses on the functioning of the intervention and serves primarily to determine whether beneficiaries have actually benefited from their activities. Results are usually evaluated by assessing whether there is a change between the start and the end of the intervention or between at least two specific time periods. Ideally, this change should be attributed to the actions taken. The main issues identified by the evaluation are as follows Has our activity made a measurable difference in our target groups? How many changes can we observe in our functions? What has contributed to our success or our failure? Can we look at the changes that have been observed? Copy to other environments? Did we get an impact on a profitable path? Do you have unexpected results? At the start of the program, it is important to obtain baseline cash flow data that will be used to compare the progress of each evaluation period and at the end of the program period. When thinking about how to measure results the changes that have been made, consider the following key points Understand how inputs, outputs, activities, etc. change. Develop your evaluation plan i.e., research plan before starting or intervening in the program. Use the results linked to your beneficiaries. Use data collection methods adapted to the needs of beneficiaries and the skills of your staff. Encourage beneficiaries to provide you with data on key inventories. Make sure you have the right data management and analysis tools and people who know how to use them. When effective, the benefits of implementing the application will be monitored and evaluated by stakeholders above and below the scope of the organization involved. In general, it guides strategic decision making during and after program implementation. Benefits for various stakeholders, such as Beneficiaries Monitoring procedures data collection can mean that the organization is really interested in results and improves results. The data can be used to improve the efficiency of the application and to improve the design of the application to improve beneficiary outcomes. Employees M&E can build resources and confidence in an organization's commitment to a mission when it is clear that it will not only assess progress, but use that assessment to have better impact. For employees who come into contact with beneficiaries e.g.: "onsite", carrying out appraisal assessments can also build trust between these employees and the community of beneficiaries. Now, often in unpredictable ways, information can emerge, helping employees discover new, more effective ways to deliver programs and create impact. Executive direction determining the strategic direction of change is done much more on the basis of data and analysis of M&E processes. The point becomes ideally agile. Managers with relevant and integrated data related to process and impact can make much more convincing arguments. Donors' Cash flow data and good M&E implementation can open that flow, as it has had an impact on credibility and, of course, a more transparent understanding of impact than an investment per dollar can have.

The Role of Monitoring and Evaluation:

Monitoring and evaluation serve multiple purposes in program management:

Assessing program effectiveness: M&E helps determine whether a program is achieving its intended outcomes and objectives. By collecting data on program activities, outputs, and outcomes, organizations can measure progress and identify areas for improvement. This assessment enables evidence-based decision-making and supports program refinement.

Monitoring program costs: M&E allows organizations to track program costs and resource utilization. By analyzing expenditure patterns, organizations can ensure the efficient allocation of resources and identify opportunities for cost optimization.

Facilitating informed decision-making: The data and insights generated through M&E provide stakeholders with the necessary information to make informed decisions. This includes decisions related to program adjustments, resource allocation, and strategic planning.

Enhancing accountability: M&E promotes transparency and accountability by providing evidence of program performance. It allows organizations to demonstrate their impact to stakeholders, donors, and the wider community.

Integrating Monitoring and Evaluation into Program Design:

To maximize the effectiveness of M&E, it should be integrated into the program design from the outset. This involves considering the data needs and indicators required to measure progress and outcomes. By identifying key performance indicators and data collection methods during the program planning phase, organizations can ensure that monitoring and evaluation efforts are aligned with program objectives. Additionally, establishing a robust data management system and building the necessary capacity within the organization for data collection, analysis, and utilization are essential components of effective M&E.

Monitoring and evaluation are vital components of program management that enable organizations to assess program effectiveness, track progress, and make informed decisions. By embracing a continuous monitoring approach and integrating M&E into program design, organizations can gather valuable data, measure outcomes, and identify areas for improvement. Surveillance allows for ongoing tracking of activities and ensures that programs remain on course. Furthermore, comprehensive planning and resource allocation are crucial for successful M&E implementation. By leveraging the power of M&E, organizations can enhance program outcomes, increase accountability, and drive positive change.

Enhancing Program Evaluation:

Maximizing Impact and Accountability:

Program evaluation plays a crucial role in assessing the effectiveness of interventions and determining whether beneficiaries have truly benefited from them. Evaluating results involves examining changes over time and attributing them to the actions taken. This article emphasizes the importance of program evaluation and explores key questions to consider when evaluating program impact. Additionally, it highlights the benefits of effective evaluation for various stakeholders, including beneficiaries, employees, executive leadership, and donors. By implementing robust evaluation practices, organizations can enhance their programs, make evidence-based decisions, and ensure accountability.

Evaluating Program Impact:

Program evaluation focuses on assessing the impact of interventions by measuring changes in the target groups. Key questions that arise during evaluation include:

- Has our activity made a measurable difference in our target groups?

- How many changes can we observe in our functions?
- What factors have contributed to our success or failure?
- Can the observed changes be replicated in other environments?
- Have we achieved a sustainable impact?
- Have any unexpected results emerged?

Measuring Results and Changes:

To measure results and changes, it is essential to establish baseline data at the start of the program. This baseline data serves as a comparison point for evaluating progress during different evaluation periods. When considering how to measure results and changes, the following key points should be considered:

- Understand how inputs, outputs, and activities contribute to changes.
- Develop an evaluation plan or research plan before program implementation.
- Utilize results that are relevant and meaningful to beneficiaries.

- Use data collection methods that are tailored to the needs of beneficiaries and the capabilities of the staff.
- Encourage beneficiaries to provide data on key indicators.
- Ensure the availability of appropriate data management and analysis tools, along with skilled personnel to utilize them effectively.

Benefits for Stakeholders:

Effective implementation of program evaluation yields benefits for various stakeholders involved in the program:

Beneficiaries: Monitoring and data collection demonstrate the organization's commitment to achieving results and improving outcomes for beneficiaries. The data collected can be used to enhance program efficiency and inform program design to better serve beneficiary needs.

Employees: Program evaluation fosters a sense of purpose and confidence among employees, as they witness the organization's commitment to assessing progress and utilizing evaluation findings to create meaningful impact. It also builds trust between employees and the beneficiary community, leading to the discovery of innovative and effective program delivery approaches.

Executive Leadership: Program evaluation provides valuable data and analysis to inform strategic decision-making. With comprehensive information on processes and impact, executives can make informed arguments and drive agile decision-making within the organization.

Donors: Robust evaluation practices, backed by cash flow data, enhance credibility, transparency, and accountability. Donors are more likely to support programs that demonstrate a clear understanding of their impact and provide evidence of their effectiveness.

Program evaluation is a critical component of effective program management, enabling organizations to assess impact, improve outcomes, and ensure accountability. By asking the right questions, measuring results, and embracing tailored evaluation methodologies, organizations can gain valuable insights into program effectiveness. Furthermore, effective evaluation practices benefit stakeholders by enhancing program efficiency, building trust, and informing strategic decision-making. By prioritizing program evaluation and utilizing evaluation findings, organizations can maximize their impact, improve program delivery, and create positive change for their beneficiaries.

Enhancing Learning and Accountability in Monitoring, Evaluation, and Accountability

Learning is a crucial outcome of Monitoring, Evaluation, and Accountability (MEA) processes within the NGO sector. The focus on learning has led to the emergence of specialized professionals in MEA, emphasizing the importance of effectively integrating learning into these processes. Learning and accountability, although distinct, share a complex relationship and are often intertwined in the goals of activities. This article explores the significance of learning in MEA, particularly in relation to responsibility and accountability. Furthermore, it proposes a revised conception of learning to enhance fiscal policies and improve program outcomes.

Learning

One of the most important outcomes of the Monitoring Evaluation and Accountability is the Learn this includes Lesson Learned and Success Stories. With so much talk about learning in the NGO sector, it is becoming more and more important to have professional Monitoring Evaluation Accountability and Learn specialists. Learning, with particular emphasis on monitoring and evaluation M&E processes can contribute to and support effective containment. Learning and responsibility are using different powers complicate their relationship. Once the assessment conditions are defined, it is common to see responsibility and learning reflected in the common goals of the activity. In fact, these two goals are common inappropriate. The challenge for those of us who approach learning from an M&E perspective is to ensure that it remains a key outcome, embedded in both process and product evaluation. When considering responsibility for the use of inputs Carry out activities to achieve results or outcomes; it becomes clearer that accountability gives us a set of facts and information that we need to analyze in order to learn. Considering the development intervention at the level of the conceptual and problematic statement, it is clear that any development project or program is based on a hypothesis. We understand how we apply them. Learning is clearly an integral part of the process of reviewing the suitability of this case and its application. To integrate learning and accountability, we need to ask different questions about inputs, activities, outcomes, outcomes and impacts at each level. In recent decades, Western development chambers have relied on rigorous evaluations and sound policies to respond to global skepticism about aid effectiveness. The resulting rhetoric sees "accountability" and "learning" as two pillars that will ensure a more effective aid system. This contribution questions the capacity of these concepts to enhance support in their current forms of work. The contribution proposes a revised conception of learning to improve fiscal and financial policies. The revised definition supports two specific areas where 'learning' is essential but avoided in the most recent institutionalized assessments developing a theory of social change (such as gender-based violence theories) and evaluating outcomes, process of designing and implementing projects as participatory projects. Some specialists see "evaluation" as a tool for program managers rather than a tool for a broader assessment of the results and impact of external assistance. However, with somewhat different approaches, systematic learning efforts can be used by various stakeholders to monitor and evaluate activities directly related to frontline leaders.

Learning and Responsibility

Maximizing Aid Effectiveness through Integrated MEA

In recent years, the importance of accountability and learning in improving aid effectiveness has gained significant recognition. However, to fully maximize the potential of these concepts, it is crucial to revisit and redefine our current conceptions of learning within the context of Monitoring, Evaluation, and Accountability (MEA). This article explores new perspectives and ideas to enhance learning in MEA, emphasizing the interconnectedness of learning and responsibility. It delves into the integration of learning into the evaluation process, the development of comprehensive theories of social change, the evaluation of participatory projects, the broader application of learning for various stakeholders, and the enhancement of fiscal policies through learning.

Integration of Learning into the Evaluation Process:

Learning is an intrinsic outcome of the MEA process. It is essential to embed learning mechanisms throughout the evaluation process, ensuring that it is not treated as an afterthought but as an integral part of the evaluation itself. By actively integrating learning into the evaluation process, organizations can systematically capture insights, gather evidence, and analyze data to generate actionable knowledge. This knowledge can then inform decision-making, program design, and future interventions, promoting adaptive management and continuous improvement.

Developing Comprehensive Theories of Social Change: The current institutionalized assessments often overlook the importance of developing comprehensive theories of social change, especially in areas such as gender-based violence. To address this gap, organizations should prioritize the integration of robust learning mechanisms into the assessment process. By embracing a theory-driven approach to social change, organizations can gain a deeper understanding of the complex dynamics at play, identify contextual factors that influence outcomes, and design interventions that address the root causes of social issues. This comprehensive understanding enables organizations to implement more targeted and effective strategies, leading to sustainable change.

Evaluating Participatory Projects: Participatory projects provide a unique opportunity for stakeholders to actively engage in the design, implementation, and evaluation processes. However, the evaluation of outcomes and the learning potential within these projects are often neglected. It is crucial to integrate learning as a core component of participatory projects, ensuring that stakeholders have a voice in the evaluation process. By incorporating participatory learning approaches, organizations can foster greater stakeholder engagement, improve project design, and ensure more impactful outcomes. This involves creating safe spaces for dialogue, encouraging reflection, and co-creating knowledge with diverse stakeholders.

Learning as a Tool for Various Stakeholders: While evaluation is often viewed primarily as a program management tool, its scope extends beyond that. Learning efforts can be leveraged to engage various stakeholders, including frontline leaders, beneficiaries, policymakers, and funders. By involving multiple stakeholders in the learning process, organizations can foster a sense of ownership, mutual accountability, and shared responsibility. This promotes transparency, strengthens partnerships, and enhances the overall effectiveness of interventions. Additionally, frontline leaders and beneficiaries, as key actors, can contribute valuable insights, perspectives, and local knowledge, enriching the learning process and leading to more contextually relevant intervention.

Enhancing Fiscal Policies through Learning: Rigorous evaluations and sound fiscal policies have been important responses to global skepticism about aid effectiveness. However, to further enhance fiscal policies, it is essential to integrate learning into their design and implementation. By incorporating learning as a fundamental component of fiscal policies, organizations can create feedback loops that facilitate evidence-based decision-making and adaptive management. This iterative process enables organizations to refine their approaches, reallocate resources based on lessons learned, and maximize the efficiency and impact of their interventions.

Learning is a vital component of MEA processes, enabling organizations to adapt, improve, and achieve better outcomes. By recognizing the interconnectedness of learning and responsibility, organizations can foster a culture of continuous improvement, evidence-based decision-making, and shared accountability. Revisiting and redefining the current conceptions of learning and integrating it into various stages of program implementation, including participatory projects and theories of social change, enhances the effectiveness of interventions. Furthermore, by utilizing learning as a tool for multiple stakeholders and incorporating it into fiscal policies, organizations can maximize the impact of their efforts and navigate the evolving landscape of aid effectiveness with agility and effectiveness. By embracing these ideas and approaches, organizations can truly harness the transformative power of MEA.

The Role of AMEL in Sustainable Development:

Unveiling the Pillars of Sustainable Development

Sustainable development has emerged as a critical global agenda, aiming to create a better future for both the present and future generations. It encompasses the harmonious integration of economic growth, social progress, and environmental protection. To achieve sustainable development, it is vital to understand the pillars that support this transformative journey.

At its core, sustainable development rests upon three interconnected pillars: economic development, social inclusion, and environmental sustainability. These pillars are intricately woven together, forming the foundation for a balanced and resilient society.

The first pillar, economic development, focuses on fostering inclusive and sustainable economic growth. It entails promoting productivity, innovation, and entrepreneurship while ensuring equitable distribution of resources and opportunities. Economic development seeks to eradicate poverty, create decent jobs, and enhance living standards. It recognizes the importance of sustainable consumption and production patterns, as well as the prudent management of natural resources.

The second pillar, social inclusion, emphasizes the fair and just treatment of all individuals within society. It seeks to eliminate inequalities, discrimination, and social exclusion. Social inclusion encompasses access to quality education, healthcare, housing, and basic services for all. It recognizes the rights of marginalized groups, promotes gender equality, and strives for social justice. By fostering inclusive societies, social inclusion contributes to social cohesion, stability, and well-being.

The third pillar, environmental sustainability, acknowledges the finite nature of our planet's resources and the need to protect and preserve them for future generations. It entails the responsible stewardship of ecosystems and biodiversity, the mitigation of climate change, and the promotion of renewable energy sources. Environmental sustainability also encompasses sustainable agriculture, water management, waste reduction, and pollution prevention. By safeguarding the environment, we ensure the long-term viability of our natural resources and the resilience of ecosystems that support life.

These three pillars are interconnected and mutually reinforcing. Economic development facilitates social inclusion by providing opportunities for individuals to thrive. Social inclusion, in turn, nurtures a more equitable society where all individuals can contribute to and benefit from development. Environmental sustainability, on the other hand, underpins both economic development and social inclusion by preserving the natural resources and ecological systems upon which they rely.

To achieve sustainable development, it is crucial to adopt an integrated and holistic approach. This involves recognizing the interdependencies between economic, social, and environmental aspects of development and addressing them in a coordinated manner. It requires the active participation and collaboration of governments, civil society, businesses, and individuals.

Furthermore, achieving sustainable development necessitates robust Accountability, Monitoring, Evaluation and Learning (AMEL) mechanisms. These mechanisms help track progress, assess the impact of interventions, ensure transparency and accountability, and foster continuous learning and improvement. AMEL provides a feedback loop that enables stakeholders to refine strategies, make evidence-based decisions, and adapt interventions to changing circumstances.

sustainable development stands on the pillars of economic development, social inclusion, and environmental sustainability. These pillars are interconnected and reinforce one another. By embracing these principles and adopting an integrated approach, we can pave the way for a future where prosperity, equality, and environmental stewardship coexist. It is through these collective efforts that we can unveil the true potential of sustainable development and build a better world for generations to come.

The Interplay of Accountability, Monitoring, Evaluation and Learning in Sustainable Development

Accountability, Monitoring, Evaluation and Learning (AMEL) are integral components of sustainable development. AMEL mechanisms provide a framework for tracking progress, assessing impact, ensuring transparency and accountability, and fostering continuous learning and improvement. In this article, we will explore the interplay of Accountability, Monitoring, Evaluation and Learning in the context of sustainable development, highlighting their importance and providing insights into designing effective AMEL systems. Additionally, we will examine case studies that demonstrate the practical application of monitoring for sustainable development.

Monitoring for Sustainable Development

Monitoring plays a crucial role in sustainable development by providing a systematic and structured approach to track progress towards achieving development goals. It involves the collection, analysis, and interpretation of data to assess the implementation of programs, projects, and policies. Monitoring enables stakeholders to identify bottlenecks, measure results, and make evidence-based decisions to ensure that development efforts are on track.

The Importance of Monitoring: Tracking Progress and Assessing Impact

Monitoring is essential for tracking progress and assessing the impact of sustainable development initiatives. It allows stakeholders to measure the effectiveness and efficiency of interventions, identify areas of success and improvement, and make informed decisions regarding resource allocation and policy adjustments. By monitoring key indicators and targets, organizations can ensure that their activities are aligned with their intended outcomes and make necessary adjustments to achieve desired results.

Designing Effective Monitoring Systems:

Indicators, Data Collection, and Analysis

Designing effective monitoring systems requires careful consideration of indicators, data collection methods, and analysis techniques. Indicators serve as measurable parameters that reflect progress towards sustainable development goals. They should be specific, measurable, achievable, relevant, and time-bound (SMART) to ensure clarity and consistency in monitoring efforts.

Data collection methods can vary depending on the nature of the indicators and the available resources. These methods can include surveys, interviews, focus groups, observations, and the use of existing data sources. It is crucial to ensure data quality and reliability through rigorous sampling techniques, data validation processes, and adherence to ethical standards.

Once data is collected, it needs to be analyzed and interpreted to derive meaningful insights. Data analysis techniques can range from simple descriptive statistics to more advanced statistical modeling and data visualization. The analysis should be conducted in a way that allows for comparisons, trend analysis, and identification of patterns and correlations.

Case Studies in Monitoring for Sustainable Development

The Millennium Development Goals (MDGs): The MDGs, a set of global development goals adopted in 2000, provided a framework for monitoring progress in areas such as poverty reduction, education, gender equality, and environmental sustainability. Monitoring efforts focused on tracking indicators and targets, allowing stakeholders to measure progress, identify gaps, and mobilize resources to accelerate achievement.

The Sustainable Development Goals (SDGs): The SDGs, adopted in 2015, build upon the MDGs and provide a comprehensive framework for sustainable development. Monitoring efforts for the SDGs involve tracking a wide range of indicators across various sectors, including poverty, health, education, climate action, and sustainable cities. The SDG indicators serve as a roadmap for monitoring progress at the global, national, and local levels.

The Global Reporting Initiative (GRI): The GRI, an international standard for sustainability reporting, provides organizations with a framework to monitor and report on their environmental, social, and governance (ESG) performance. By monitoring key ESG indicators, organizations can identify areas for improvement, demonstrate accountability to stakeholders, and drive sustainability efforts.

Accountability, Monitoring, Evaluation and Learning are crucial components of sustainable development. By implementing effective AMEL mechanisms, stakeholders can track progress, assess impact, ensure transparency and accountability, and foster continuous learning and improvement. The interplay of Accountability, Monitoring, Evaluation and Learning provides a comprehensive framework for achieving sustainable development goals. Through case studies, we have seen how monitoring efforts have been applied in the context of the Millennium Development Goals, the Sustainable Development Goals, and sustainability reporting. By embracing these AMEL practices, we can navigate the path towards a more sustainable and equitable future.

Evaluation as a Catalyst for Sustainable Development

Evaluation plays a crucial role in driving sustainable development by providing valuable insights into the effectiveness, efficiency, and impact of programs and initiatives. It enables stakeholders to make informed decisions, improve program design and implementation, and ensure accountability. In this article, we will explore the significance of evaluation in sustainable development, delve into various methods and approaches for evaluating sustainable development programs, discuss how evaluation results can inform decision-making and improve effectiveness, and examine real-life examples of evaluation in sustainable development initiatives.

Evaluating Sustainable Development Programs:

Methods, Approaches, and Frameworks

Evaluating sustainable development programs requires a systematic and rigorous approach to assess their performance and impact. Various methods and approaches can be employed to gather data, analyze information, and derive meaningful insights. Some commonly used evaluation methods in sustainable development include:

Impact Evaluation: Impact evaluation aims to determine the causal effects of a program or intervention on desired outcomes. It involves comparing outcomes between a group that receives the intervention and a comparison group that does not. Randomized controlled trials (RCTs), quasi-experimental designs, and before-and-after studies are commonly used approaches in impact evaluation.

Outcome Evaluation: Outcome evaluation focuses on measuring the intended results or outcomes of a program. It involves assessing whether the program has achieved its objectives and the extent to which it has contributed to desired outcomes. Outcome evaluation often employs quantitative and qualitative data collection methods, such as surveys, interviews, and document analysis.

Process Evaluation: Process evaluation examines the implementation of a program, including its fidelity, adherence to the planned activities, and the quality of program delivery. It helps identify barriers and facilitators to program implementation and provides insights into the context in which the program operates. Process evaluation often involves observations, interviews, and document reviews.

Frameworks such as the Logical Framework Approach (LFA), Results-Based Management (RBM), and Theory of Change (ToC) provide structures for designing and conducting evaluations in sustainable development. These frameworks help define program goals, outcomes, indicators, and the relationships between inputs, activities, outputs, and outcomes.

Utilizing Evaluation Results:

Informing Decision-Making and Improving Effectiveness

The value of evaluation lies not only in assessing program performance but also in utilizing the findings to inform decision-making and improve program effectiveness. Evaluation results can be used in the following ways:

Evidence-Based Decision-Making: Evaluation findings provide evidence that supports decision-making processes. They offer insights into what works, what doesn't, and why. Policymakers, program managers, and stakeholders can use evaluation results to make informed decisions about resource allocation, program adjustments, and policy formulation.

Learning and Adaptation: Evaluation promotes learning and continuous improvement. By examining the strengths and weaknesses of a program, stakeholders can identify areas for improvement and make necessary adjustments. Evaluation results can inform program refinements, capacity-building efforts, and strategic planning to ensure that programs are responsive to changing needs and contexts.

Accountability and Transparency: Evaluation enhances accountability and transparency in sustainable development initiatives. By conducting independent and objective evaluations, stakeholders can demonstrate their commitment to monitoring program performance and ensuring that resources are used effectively and efficiently. Evaluation reports can be shared with stakeholders, fostering transparency and building trust.

Real-Life Examples of Evaluation in Sustainable Development Initiatives

The Evaluation of the Millennium Development Goals (MDGs): The MDGs: a set of global development goals, were evaluated to assess progress, identify gaps, and inform the formulation of the Sustainable Development Goals (SDGs). The evaluation of the MDGs provided valuable insights into the achievements and challenges of the global development agenda, guiding the development of the SDGs.

The Evaluation of Renewable Energy Programs: Evaluating renewable energy programs helps assess their impact on reducing greenhouse gas emissions, increasing energy access, and promoting sustainable development. These evaluations provide insights into the effectiveness of different renewable energy technologies, policy frameworks, and financing mechanisms, informing the scaling up of successful initiatives.

The Evaluation of Community-Based Conservation Projects: Evaluating community-based conservation projects helps assess their contribution to biodiversity conservation, poverty reduction, and community empowerment. These evaluations provide insights into the effectiveness of participatory approaches, community engagement strategies, and the integration of traditional knowledge in conservation efforts.

Evaluation serves as a catalyst for sustainable development by providing valuable insights into program performance, informing decision-making, and fostering continuous improvement. Through various methods, approaches, and frameworks, evaluation enables stakeholders to assess the impact of sustainable development programs and initiatives. By utilizing evaluation results, stakeholders can make evidence-based decisions, learn from successes and failures, and ensure accountability and transparency. Real-life examples demonstrate the importance of evaluation in shaping global development agendas, evaluating renewable energy programs, and assessing community-based conservation projects. As sustainable development continues to be a global priority, evaluation will play a crucial role in driving progress and achieving long-term sustainability goals.

Accountability for Sustainable Development

In recent years, the concept of accountability has gained significant importance in the context of sustainable development. As the world faces pressing environmental, social, and economic challenges, it is crucial to ensure that efforts towards sustainable development are accountable and transparent. This article will delve into the significance of accountability, the mechanisms for accountability, and showcase examples of accountability in sustainable development efforts.

The Significance of Accountability: Transparency, Responsibility, and Trust

Accountability is a fundamental principle in sustainable development that encompasses transparency, responsibility, and trust. It refers to the obligation of individuals, organizations, and governments to take responsibility for their actions, decisions, and the impact they have on the environment and society.

Transparency is a key element of accountability, as it ensures that information about sustainable development efforts, including goals, progress, and outcomes, is accessible to stakeholders. This transparency allows for meaningful engagement and participation from various actors, fostering a sense of responsibility and trust among them.

Accountability also plays a crucial role in maintaining the integrity of sustainable development initiatives. It ensures that commitments made towards achieving sustainable development goals are honored and that progress is measured and reported accurately. Without accountability, there is a risk of greenwashing, where organizations claim to be sustainable without actually making substantial progress towards sustainability.

Mechanisms for Accountability: Stakeholder Engagement and Reporting

Stakeholder Engagement: One of the primary mechanisms for accountability in sustainable development is stakeholder engagement. Stakeholders include individuals, communities, non-governmental organizations (NGOs), businesses, and governments who are affected by or have an interest in sustainable development initiatives. Engaging with stakeholders allows for their perspectives, concerns, and inputs to be considered in decision-making processes.

Stakeholder engagement can take various forms, such as public consultations, participatory workshops, and multi-stakeholder dialogues. These platforms provide opportunities for stakeholders to voice their opinions, contribute their expertise, and hold decision-makers accountable for their actions. By involving stakeholders in the decision-making process, accountability is strengthened, and sustainable development efforts become more inclusive and representative of diverse perspectives.

Reporting: Another essential mechanism for accountability in sustainable development is reporting. Reporting involves the systematic collection, analysis, and disclosure of information about sustainability performance and progress towards goals. It provides a transparent and standardized way to communicate the impact and outcomes of sustainable development efforts to stakeholders.

There are several reporting frameworks and standards that organizations can adopt to ensure accountability. The Global Reporting Initiative (GRI) and the Sustainability Accounting Standards Board (SASB) are two widely recognized frameworks that guide organizations in reporting their sustainability performance. These frameworks provide guidelines for reporting on various aspects of sustainability, including environmental impact, social responsibility, and governance practices.

Reporting not only helps organizations track their progress but also enables stakeholders to assess their commitment to sustainable development. It allows for a better understanding of the challenges, achievements, and areas for improvement, fostering a culture of accountability and continuous learning.

Showcasing Accountability in Sustainable Development Efforts

There are numerous examples of accountability in sustainable development efforts across the globe. Let's examine a few notable examples:

The United Nations Sustainable Development Goals (SDGs): The SDGs are a set of 17 goals established by the United Nations to address global challenges, including poverty, inequality, climate change, and sustainable consumption. The SDGs promote accountability by encouraging member states to report on their progress towards achieving the goals. Regular reviews and reporting mechanisms ensure that countries remain accountable for their commitments and identify areas where additional efforts are required.

Renewable Energy Certification Programs: Certification programs for renewable energy sources, such as wind and solar power, play a vital role in ensuring accountability. These programs provide independent verification of the environmental attributes of renewable energy generation, such as its carbon footprint and contribution to reducing greenhouse gas emissions. By obtaining certification, renewable energy providers demonstrate their accountability and commitment to sustainable energy production.

Corporate Social Responsibility (CSR) Reporting: Many companies now publish CSR reports to showcase their commitment to sustainable development. These reports disclose information about the company's environmental impact, labor practices, community engagement, and governance structures. By voluntarily reporting on their sustainability performance, companies demonstrate their accountability to stakeholders and foster transparency and trust.

Accountability is a critical aspect of sustainable development, ensuring transparency, responsibility, and trust among stakeholders. Mechanisms such as stakeholder engagement and reporting play a crucial role in fostering accountability and ensuring that sustainable development efforts are effective and impactful. By showcasing accountability in sustainable development initiatives, we can create a more sustainable and equitable future for all.

Learning for Continuous Improvement in Sustainable Development

Sustainable development is a complex and ever-evolving field that requires continuous improvement and adaptation. In order to achieve long-term sustainability goals, it is crucial to foster a culture of learning that promotes adaptation, innovation, and knowledge sharing. This article will explore the power of learning in sustainable development, the importance of creating learning cultures, and provide inspiring examples of learning in sustainable development endeavors.

The Power of Learning: Promoting Adaptation, Innovation, and Knowledge Sharing

Learning plays a pivotal role in sustainable development by facilitating adaptation to changing environmental, social, and economic conditions. It enables individuals and organizations to acquire new knowledge, skills, and perspectives that can inform and drive innovative solutions. By embracing a learning mindset, stakeholders in sustainable development can continuously improve their strategies and approaches, ensuring that they remain effective and relevant over time.

Furthermore, learning promotes knowledge sharing, enabling stakeholders to exchange experiences, best practices, and lessons learned. This collaborative approach allows for the dissemination of valuable insights and fosters cross-sectoral cooperation, enabling a more holistic and integrated approach to sustainable development. Through knowledge sharing, stakeholders can build upon each other's successes and failures, accelerating progress towards sustainability goals.

Creating Learning Cultures: Capacity Building, Collaboration, and Reflection

To harness the full potential of learning in sustainable development, it is essential to create learning cultures that prioritize capacity building, collaboration, and reflection.

Capacity building: involves providing individuals and organizations with the necessary knowledge, skills, and resources to effectively engage in sustainable development efforts. This can be achieved through training programs, workshops, and mentorship opportunities. By investing in capacity building, stakeholders can empower themselves to tackle sustainability challenges more effectively and drive positive change.

Collaboration: is another key aspect of creating learning cultures. By fostering collaboration among diverse stakeholders, such as government agencies, non-governmental organizations, businesses, and communities, knowledge and resources can be shared, and collective action can be taken. Collaborative learning allows for the co-creation of innovative solutions that address complex sustainability issues from multiple perspectives.

Reflection: is a critical component of learning cultures in sustainable development. It involves evaluating past actions, outcomes, and impacts to identify areas for improvement and inform future decision-making. Through reflection, stakeholders can learn from both successes and failures, ensuring that lessons are internalized and applied to future endeavors. Additionally, reflection encourages a culture of continuous improvement, where feedback loops are incorporated into project design and implementation.

Inspiring Examples of Learning in Sustainable Development Endeavors

Several inspiring examples of learning in sustainable development endeavors demonstrate the transformative power of a learning-focused approach:

The Sustainable Development Goals (SDGs) Learning Lab: This online platform provides resources, tools, and case studies to support learning and knowledge sharing on the SDGs. It enables stakeholders to access and contribute to a global repository of best practices, lessons learned, and innovative solutions.

The Global Learning and Observations to Benefit the Environment (GLOBE) Program: This international science and education program engages students, educators, and scientists in collecting and analyzing environmental data. By participating in hands-on learning experiences, students develop a deeper understanding of environmental issues and become actively engaged in sustainable development efforts.

The Circular Economy Learning Hub: This initiative by the Ellen MacArthur Foundation offers a range of learning materials and courses on the concept of the circular economy. It equips individuals and businesses with the knowledge and skills needed to transition towards a more sustainable and regenerative economic model.

The Learning Network for Water and Sanitation (WASH): This network brings together practitioners, researchers, and policymakers to share knowledge and experiences in the water and sanitation sector. By promoting learning and collaboration, the network contributes to improved practices and policies that enhance access to clean water and sanitation services worldwide.

Learning is a powerful tool for continuous improvement in sustainable development. By promoting adaptation, innovation, and knowledge sharing, learning enables stakeholders to address complex sustainability challenges effectively. Creating learning cultures that prioritize capacity building, collaboration, and reflection further enhances the impact of learning efforts. Inspiring examples of learning in sustainable development endeavors demonstrate the transformative potential of a learning-focused approach. As we strive towards a more sustainable future, embracing a culture of learning will be crucial in achieving long-term success in sustainable development.

Integrated Approaches:

Harmonizing Monitoring, Evaluation, Accountability, and Learning

In the field of sustainable development, it is essential to adopt integrated approaches that harmonize Accountability, Monitoring, Evaluation and Learning (AMEL) practices. By combining these elements, organizations can maximize the impact of their sustainable development efforts. This article will explore the synergies and benefits of integrating AMEL in sustainable development, discuss the challenges and considerations in implementing integrated approaches, and provide inspiring success stories of organizations that have embraced integrated AMEL approaches in their sustainable development practices.

Synergies and Integration: Maximizing the Impact of Sustainable Development Efforts

Integrating AMEL practices in sustainable development initiatives brings several synergistic benefits, ultimately maximizing the impact of these efforts.

Coherence and Alignment: Integrated AMEL approaches ensure coherence and alignment between project objectives, activities, and outcomes. By incorporating monitoring and evaluation from the outset of a project, organizations can better understand the progress being made and make timely adjustments to ensure alignment with the desired outcomes.

Continuous Learning and Adaptation: Integrating learning into the AMEL process enables organizations to continuously learn from their experiences and adapt their strategies accordingly. By collecting and analyzing data throughout the project lifecycle, organizations can identify what works and what doesn't, leading to improved decision-making and more effective interventions.

Evidence–Based Decision Making: Integrated AMEL approaches provide organizations with robust evidence to inform decision-making. By systematically collecting and analyzing data, organizations can generate evidence on the impact of their interventions, identify best practices, and make informed decisions on resource allocation and programmatic adjustments.

Accountability and Transparency: Integrating accountability mechanisms into the AMEL process enhances transparency and ensures that organizations are accountable to their stakeholders. By tracking progress, reporting on results, and engaging stakeholders in the process, organizations can build trust and demonstrate their commitment to achieving sustainable development goals.

Challenges and Considerations in Integrating AMEL in Sustainable Development

While integrating AMEL practices in sustainable development brings numerous benefits, it also presents challenges that organizations must address for successful implementation.

Capacity Building: Integrating AMEL requires organizations to build the capacity of their staff in monitoring, evaluation, and learning methodologies.

This may involve training in data collection, analysis, and interpretation, as well as fostering a culture of learning and reflection within the organization.

Data Management and Analysis: Integrating AMEL involves collecting, managing, and analyzing large volumes of data. Organizations need to invest in robust data management systems, ensure data quality and security, and have the analytical capacity to derive meaningful insights from the data collected.

Stakeholder Engagement: Integrated AMEL approaches require active engagement and participation from multiple stakeholders, including beneficiaries, local communities, and other relevant actors. Organizations must invest in building strong relationships, fostering trust, and ensuring meaningful participation throughout the AMEL process.

Resource Constraints: Integrating AMEL practices may require additional resources, including financial, human, and technological. Organizations need to carefully plan and allocate resources to support the implementation of integrated AMEL approaches, ensuring sustainability and long-term impact.

Success Stories of Integrated AMEL Approaches in Sustainable Development Practice

Several organizations have successfully embraced integrated AMEL approaches in their sustainable development practices, demonstrating the transformative potential of these approaches.

The United Nations Development Programme (UNDP): The UNDP has adopted an integrated AMEL framework that incorporates Accountability, Monitoring, Evaluation and Learning into its programs. By systematically tracking progress, evaluating outcomes, and promoting learning, the UNDP has been able to enhance the effectiveness of its development interventions and improve results for sustainable development.

Oxfam: Oxfam has implemented an integrated AMEL system that focuses on participatory approaches and accountability. By actively involving communities and stakeholders in the monitoring and evaluation process, Oxfam ensures that programs are responsive to local needs and priorities. This approach has led to increased community ownership and sustainability of development initiatives.

The World Bank: The World Bank has integrated AMEL into its projects to enhance accountability and learning. Through rigorous monitoring and evaluation, the World Bank has been able to identify successful approaches, scale up interventions, and continuously improve its programs to achieve better development outcomes.

The Global Fund to Fight AIDS, Tuberculosis, and Malaria: The Global Fund has integrated AMEL as a core component of its grant-making process. By monitoring and evaluating the impact of funded programs, the Global Fund ensures accountability and drives evidence-based decision-making to maximize the impact of investments in health interventions.

Integrated approaches that harmonize Accountability, Monitoring, Evaluation and Learning (AMEL) are essential for maximizing the impact of sustainable development efforts. By embracing integrated AMEL approaches, organizations can ensure coherence and alignment, promote continuous learning and adaptation, make evidence-based decisions, and enhance accountability and transparency. While there are challenges in implementing integrated AMEL approaches, numerous success stories demonstrate their transformative potential. Organizations such as the UNDP, Oxfam, the World Bank, and the Global Fund have successfully integrated AMEL into their sustainable development practices, leading to improved outcomes and increased effectiveness. By learning from these success stories and addressing the challenges, organizations can embrace integrated AMEL approaches and make a lasting impact on sustainable development.

Recommended Resources:

Further Readings on AMEL and Sustainable Development

Accountability, Monitoring, Evaluation and Learning (AMEL) is a vital framework in the field of sustainable development. It plays a crucial role in ensuring the effectiveness and impact of development projects and programs. Sustainable development, on the other hand, focuses on meeting the needs of the present without compromising the ability of future generations to meet their own needs. In this article, we will provide a comprehensive list of recommended resources for further reading on MEAL and sustainable development. These resources will help deepen your understanding of the concepts, tools, and practices related to MEAL and sustainable development.

Books

1. "Monitoring and Evaluation Training: A Systematic Approach" by Mohamad Hasan Mohaqeq Moein: This book offers a comprehensive guide to the principles and practices of monitoring and

evaluation. It covers various topics, including project planning, data collection and analysis, and reporting. It is suitable for both beginners and experienced professionals in the field of MEAL.

2. "Evaluation: A Systematic Approach" by Peter H. Rossi, Mark W. Lipsey, and Howard E. Freeman: This classic book provides a thorough introduction to evaluation methodologies and techniques. It offers practical guidance on conducting evaluations, including designing evaluation studies, collecting and analyzing data, and reporting findings. It is a valuable resource for those interested in understanding the evaluation process.

3. "Sustainable Development Goals: Their Impacts on Forests and People" edited by Pia Katila, Glenn Galloway, Wil de Jong, Pablo Pacheco, and Gerardo Mery: This book explores the relationship between the Sustainable Development Goals (SDGs) and forests. It examines the role of forests in achieving the SDGs and provides insights into the challenges and opportunities associated with sustainable forest management. It is a must-read for those interested in the intersection of sustainable development and natural resources.

4. "Evaluation for a Caring Society" by Michael Quinn Patton: This book explores the role of evaluation in promoting social justice and equity. It presents a framework for conducting evaluations that are responsive to the needs and values of diverse stakeholders. It is a thought-provoking resource for

those interested in incorporating social justice principles into their evaluation practice.

Reports and Publications

1. The United Nations Sustainable Development Goals Knowledge Platform: This online platform provides access to a wide range of reports, publications, and resources related to the Sustainable Development Goals. It offers in-depth information on each of the goals, including their targets and indicators. It is a valuable resource for understanding the global agenda for sustainable development.
2. The World Bank Group's Independent Evaluation Group (IEG) Publications: The IEG produces a range of reports and publications on evaluation in the context of international development. Their publications cover various topics, including project evaluations, thematic evaluations, and methodological guidance. They provide insights into best practices and lessons learned in the field of evaluation.
3. The MEAL DPro Network Resources: The MEAL DPro Network is a global community of professionals working in the field of MEAL. Their website offers a collection of resources, including case studies, toolkits, and guidelines. These resources provide practical insights into implementing MEAL frameworks and approaches in different contexts.

4. The OECD Development Assistance Committee (DAC) Evaluation Resource Center: The DAC Evaluation Resource Center provides access to a wealth of evaluation-related resources. Their publications cover topics such as evaluation methods, evaluation capacity development, and evaluation criteria. They offer valuable insights for practitioners and policymakers involved in development evaluation.

Academic Journals

1. "Evaluation and Program Planning": This academic journal focuses on the theory and practice of evaluation in the social sciences. It publishes research articles, case studies, and methodological papers related to evaluation. It is a valuable resource for staying updated on the latest developments in the field of evaluation.
2. "Sustainability Science": This interdisciplinary journal focuses on research related to sustainable development. It covers topics such as sustainable resource management, social equity, and climate change adaptation. It publishes original research articles, reviews, and policy analyses. It is a valuable resource for those interested in the intersection of sustainability and development.
3. "Journal of Development Effectiveness": This journal publishes research articles on the effectiveness of development interventions. It covers topics such as impact evaluation, theories of change, and evidence-

based policy making. It is a valuable resource for researchers and practitioners seeking to understand the impact of development programs and policies.

4. "Evaluation Review": This journal focuses on the theory and practice of evaluation in various fields, including education, health, and social services. It publishes research articles, literature reviews, and methodological papers. It is a valuable resource for those interested in evaluation theory and practice.

Online Courses and Training Programs

1. "Introduction to Monitoring and Evaluation" - Coursera: This online course provides a comprehensive introduction to monitoring and evaluation. It covers topics such as program theory, data collection and analysis, and reporting. It is offered by the University of Washington and is suitable for beginners in the field of MEAL.
2. "Sustainable Development: The Post-COVID-19 World" - edX: This online course explores the concept of sustainable development in the context of the post-COVID-19 world. It covers topics such as climate change, inequality, and sustainable cities. It is offered by the University of Queensland and is suitable for those interested in understanding the challenges and opportunities for sustainable development.
3. "Evaluation Essentials for Non-Evaluators" - American Evaluation Association: This online training program provides a comprehensive

overview of evaluation concepts and methods. It covers topics such as evaluation planning, data collection, and reporting. It is suitable for professionals who want to gain a basic understanding of evaluation principles and practices.
4. "Introduction to Sustainable Development" - Future Learn: This online course provides an introduction to the concept of sustainable development. It covers topics such as sustainable development goals, environmental sustainability, and social equity. It is offered by the University of St Andrews and is suitable for beginners in the field of sustainable development.

The resources mentioned above provide a wealth of information on MEAL and sustainable development. Whether you are a beginner looking to gain a foundational understanding or an experienced professional seeking to deepen your knowledge, these resources will help you further explore the concepts, tools, and practices in these fields. By delving into these recommended resources, you will be equipped with the necessary knowledge and insights to make a meaningful impact in the field of sustainable development.

AMEL (129)

www.ingramcontent.com/pod-product-compliance
Lightning Source LLC
Chambersburg PA
CBHW072050230526
45479CB00010B/645